People in the Community

Doctors

Diyan Leake

HEINEMANN
LIBRARY

www.heinemann.co.uk/library
Visit our website to find out more information about Heinemann Library books.

To order:
☎ Phone 44 (0) 1865 888066
🖹 Send a fax to 44 (0) 1865 314091
💻 Visit the Heinemann Bookshop at www.heinemann.co.uk/library to browse our catalogue and order online.

First published in Great Britain by Heinemann Library, Halley Court, Jordan Hill, Oxford OX2 8EJ, part of Pearson Education.
Heinemann is a registered trademark of Pearson Education Ltd.

Editorial: Diyan Leake and Catherine Clarke
Design: Joanna Hinton-Malivoire and Steve Mead
Picture research: Tracy Cummins and Heather Mauldin
Production: Alison Parsons

Origination: Chroma Graphics (Overseas) Pte Ltd
Printed and bound in China by South China Printing Company Ltd

ISBN 978 0 431 19243 7
12 11 10 09 08
10 9 8 7 6 5 4 3 2 1

British Library Cataloguing in Publication Data
Leake, Diyan
Doctors. - (People in the community)
610.6'95
A full catalogue record for this book is available from the British Library.

Acknowledgments
The publishers would like to thank the following for permission to reproduce photographs:
©Age Fotostock pp. **15** (ImageSource), **20** (John Birdsall); ©Alamy (Derrick Alderman) pp. **11**, **22 (middle)**; ©AP Photo (Bill Feig) p. **6**; ©Corbis pp. **8** (Ed Bock), **21** (Graham Bell); ©digitalrailroad.net (Keith Dannemiller) p. **5**; © Getty Images pp. **4** (Panoramic Images), **7** (Steven Peters), **9** (AFP), **10** (Somos/Veer), **12** (Siri Stafford), **13** (Andersen Ross), **14** (AFP), **16** (Pat LaCroix), **17** (Marwan Naamani/AFP), **18** (David Joel), **19** (Mike Powell), **22 (top)** (Panoramic Images), **22 (bottom)** (Mike Powell).

Front cover photograph of a doctor treating a boy in Ghana reproduced with permission of ©Corbis (Zefa/Mika). Back cover photograph reproduced with permission of ©Corbis (Graham Bell).

Every effort has been made to contact copyright holders of any material reproduced in this book. Any omissions will be rectified in subsequent printings if notice is given to the publisher.

Contents

Communities

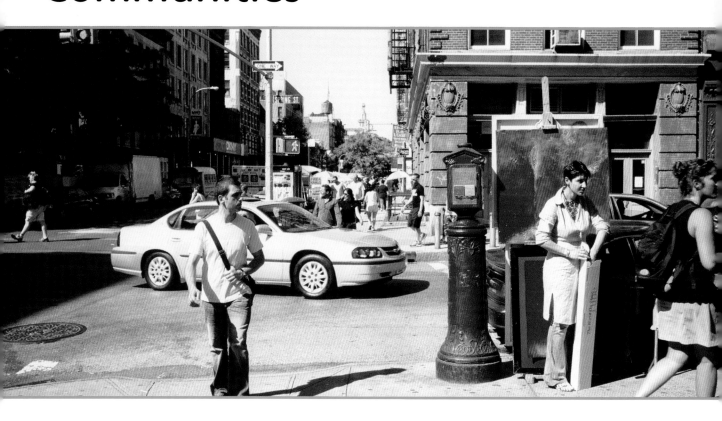

People live in communities. They live near each other and help each other.

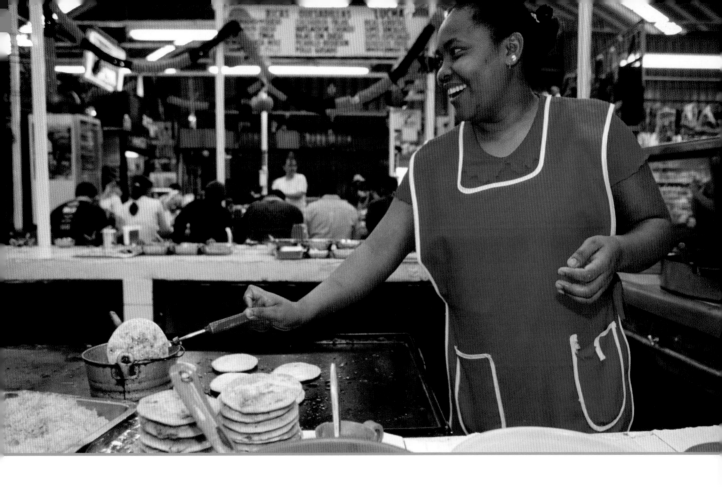

People work together in a community.

Doctors in the community

Doctors work in communities.

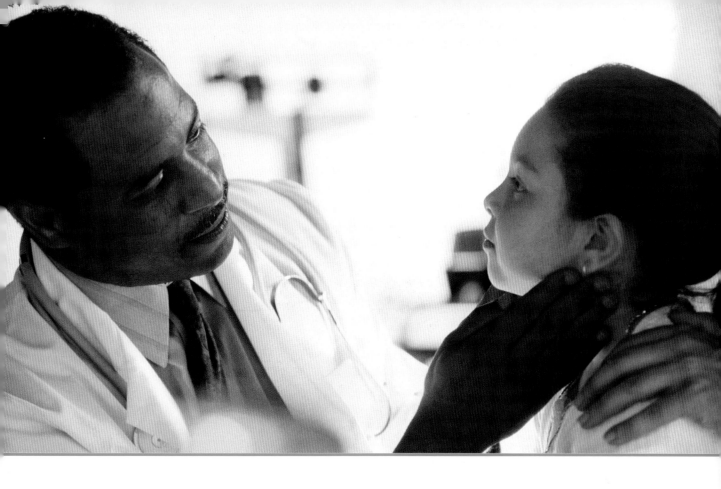

Doctors help people stay healthy.

What doctors do

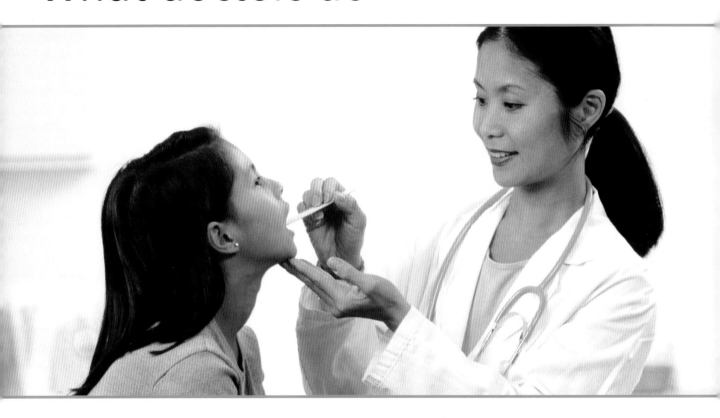

Doctors help people when they are sick.

Doctors help people when they
are hurt.

Where doctors work

Doctors work in surgeries.

Doctors work in hospitals.

What doctors wear

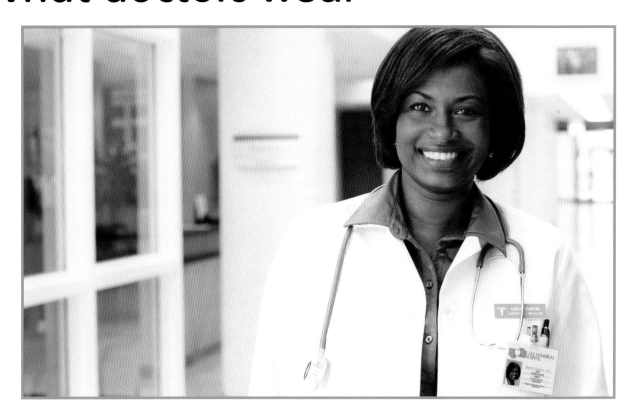

Doctors wear a white coat.

Doctors wear gloves and masks.

What doctors use

Doctors use medical kits.

Doctors use their hands.

People who work with doctors

nurse

Doctors work with nurses.

Nurses look after people.

Doctors work with paramedics.

Paramedics take people to hospital.

How doctors help us

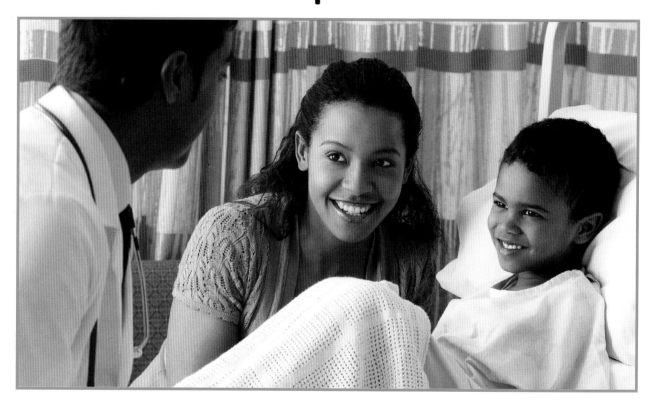

Doctors help us get better.

Doctors help the community. They keep us healthy.

Picture glossary

 community group of people living and working in the same area

 hospital place where sick or injured people are cared for by doctors and nurses

 paramedic person trained to do medical work such as first aid. Paramedics take people to hospital.

Index

Notes for parents and teachers

This series introduces readers to the lives of different community workers, and explains some of the different jobs they perform around the world. Some of the locations featured include New York, USA (page 4); Mexico City, Mexico (page 5); Baton Rouge, Los Angeles, USA (page 6); Lampedusa, Italy (page 9); Kanchanaburi, Thailand (page 14); and Beirut, Lebanon (page 17).

Before reading
Talk to the children about the work of a doctor. Ask if they have been to the doctor. Was it at a surgery or at a hospital? Did the doctor wear a white coat?
Did the doctor listen to their chest with a stethoscope or take their temperature with an ear thermometer? Did the doctor help them to feel better?

After reading
• Set up the role play area as a doctor's surgery. Give the children men's shirts to wear as white coats. Let them use the plastic instruments from a play medical kit. Be a patient yourself and ask the children to help to make you better.
• Sing the nursery rhyme: "Miss Polly had a dolly who was sick, sick, sick."
• Fold art paper in half. Ask children to draw or paint themselves feeling ill or hurt on the left-hand side (e.g. spots or a bandage on an injury). Then on the right-hand side they should draw or paint themselves feeling healthy and well.